Terms and Conditions

LEGAL NOTICE

Although the publisher made every effort to ensure that the report was as accurate and comprehensive as possible, he does not guarantee or make any representations on the accuracy of its contents at any point in time owing to the fast-evolving characteristics of the Internet.

Although every effort has been taken to confirm the information included in this publishing, the Publisher disclaims all liability for any mistakes, omissions, or opposing interpretation of the topic at hand. Any perceived slights against Unintentionally, certain individuals, groups, or entities are mentioned. Like everything else in life, there are no certainties in practical advice books about revenue generated. Readers are advised to respond based only on their assessment of their certain situations to respond appropriately.

This book is not meant to be used as a reference for legal, accounting, business, or monetary guidance. It is recommended that all readers seek the assistance of qualified experts in the domains of law, business, accounting, and finance.

For easier reading, we strongly advise you to print this book

Table Of Contents

6. **Don't Drink:** Advises against excessive alcohol consumption.

7. **Don't Blame Yourself:** Reminds readers not to be too hard on themselves.

8. **See Someone:** Encourages seeking professional help when needed.

Foreword

Are you depressed, nervous, agitated, exhausted, overwhelmed, or sensitive to emotions? These types of mood disorders are surprisingly frequent and may often be treated with ease.

The prevalence of anxiety and depression in particular has increased to the point that many people use medication for one or both of these mood disorders. In actuality, the prevalence of anxiety and depression has increased threefold since 1990, and over 25% of American adults report having one or more mood disorders.

-Escaping Depression:

Strategies for managing depression and depressive symptoms.

Chapter 1:

Journaling

The first chapter encourages keeping a journal.

Synopsis

There are times when sadness or a gloomy mood has several contributing factors and others when there is no obvious reason. Maintaining a diary is one of the most effective instruments. accessible for emotional healing and personal development. It may This ought to be a regular occurrence. Recording our opinions allows us to consider them to be distinct from ourselves.

Writing

It's possible to start doubting an idea once it's no longer seen as a component of who you are. It might be challenging to rise beyond the emotions attached to a concept when it is considered to be true. For example, a recently divorced person could believe, "I'll be I will always be alone since no one will ever love me again." Most likely, this isn't true, but the concept can seem to be so vast, genuine, and unquestionably real that The whole feeling of self is absorbed by it. Sensations of isolation and Depression descend and despair becomes deeply ingrained for the long term.

While keeping a journal just may not make depression go away, it might help loosen its hold. Maintaining a daily notebook might completely change your life. Have no fear. Exiting from Depression is worthwhile.

Some ideas to get you going:

- After getting out of bed, spend five to ten minutes doing some yoga, stretching, or exercising to get your blood flowing.
- Sip some water with a squeeze of lemon. Lack of water exacerbates fatigue and depressive symptoms. Aromas of citrus have a somewhat

euphoric effect and lemon aids in cleansing the liver.

- Ensure that your workspace is tidy and comfortable. Establish a timer. for thirty minutes, then take a seat.
- The only requirement is that you write continuously for the whole quarter-hour. Write down any thought that crosses your mind. If you get into trouble, jot down your to-do list or a lovely everything, even a memory. Just keep your hand moving.
- When the allotted time is over, shut your notepad and avoid looking at what you wrote for at least a couple of weeks.

Make sure you maintain your notepad somewhere where nobody may see it. This Written content is intended to be created, not read.

Perform this action each day.

Another activity that you may perform at any time is to start a blog to express your thankfulness to the world if you feel down. You can do this many times a day.

Just write down five or more positive aspects of your life. You may start each one by saying "I'm grateful for..." or "I'm thankful for..." because "Do you still have your health? Something for which to express gratitude. Was there a little breeze this morning? As soon as you start The amount of things for which you have gratitude will astound you. This kind of keeping a diary has a strong soothing influence on the spirit.

Chapter 2

Wellness Checklist:

This chapter provides a checklist for maintaining overall well-being.

Synopsis

A health checklist should provide sincere daily objectives to address the requirements of the mind, body, and spirit. It's not designed to drown you but to support you as you fight depression, so Make it simple.

Be Well

Adhere to a single page. Make use of a readable typeface that is "friendly" in size. Consider using a font in a soothing colour if black and white is too harsh. Every day, print a new copy of the list.

If sadness is something you're trying to overcome, your list may include the most basic everyday tasks, the things we do mindlessly while we're in good health. Wake up early, take a shower, and brush your teeth may have to be at the top of your list. Most certainly, you'll feel silly at first, crossing off such routine tasks. The idea is to remind yourself that you may overcome sadness by taking care of yourself in the most typical manner.

The items that are included will help you create your daily to-do list:

The items that are included will help you create your daily to-do list:

- Think about what you have to be grateful for when you get up.
- Engage in some exercise.
- Eat a healthy breakfast.
- Consume my vitamins
- Eat nutritious snacks.
- Get my brain working
- Ample water consumption
- Show love or service to someone today
- Consume five to seven portions of vegetables.

- Crawl into bed at a time when I can obtain enough rest.

Here's an example of a different kind of checklist. You may print this page or customize one to your specifications:

1. I am aware of what makes me tense the most. The following are some examples of tension-causing factors:

____

2. When my stress level rises, I have someone to speak to or somewhere to write. is raised My people to contact are:

____

3. I know how to relax. Calm pursuits:

____

4. I eat a variety of meals and get the nutrients I need. I have wholesome meals on hand. Healthy meals that I like:

____

5. My appetite hasn't changed much lately. Indicate if there have been any changes or not:

____

6. I engage in physical activities of some kind. Exercise routines and frequency:

____

7. I'm getting enough sleep. My sleeping patterns haven't changed much in the last several months. Add up all of your sleep and changes:

____

8. I take my medication as directed. I know what to anticipate. from my medication. Periods I've skipped taking my medication or queries I have:

____

9. I take part in social events. Among my social pursuits are:

____

10. I've told my loved ones and family about my disease to the best of my ability. List of helpful links or advice:

Chapter 3

Keep Nutrition In Check:

Practical advice on maintaining a healthy diet.

Synopsis

Having a healthy diet is essential for battling depression. This is challenging since depression often suppresses appetite. To combat sadness, you should engage in sufficient fats and calories to fuel your body and mind power.

Eat Right

When you're sad, cooking could seem like a daunting task, especially if you're not interested in eating. Making a nutritious diet as easy as possible can not only help you fight depression, but you'll also be able to say no to junk food more easily. Sugar rushes and The inevitable crashes that follow will only add to your anxiety.

To combat sadness, choose wholesome, appetizing meals that need soups, fruit, cheese, yoghurt, whole-grain cereal, and foods with little or no cooking. Even if you find it difficult to consume whole meals, you can still get a significant amount of calories each day from nutritious small meals and snacks. If you often cover up when you're sad, It is best to have wholesome snacks available for consumption. You'll be less likely to get the doughnut box.

Many depressive symptoms may have a strong correlation with vitamins and deficiencies in minerals in the typical diet, which is mostly composed of composed of sugar, coffee, and empty carbohydrates. Depression, erratic emotions, and Poor diet a common primary causes of fatigue.

Dismissing sadness or getting over a depressed episode is often as easy as changing your diet and increasing the amount of essential nutrients that contain nutrients that strengthen the brain and control brain chemistry.

Omega-3s are found in fish oils. Studies have shown that depressive People often don't have enough of the fatty acid EPA. One gramme of fish oil, just daily might result in a 50% decrease in symptoms such as anxiety and sleeplessness. disorders, inexplicable depressive sensations, thoughts of self-destruction, and a decrease in sex desire. Omega-3s may be found in flaxseed and walnuts. and fatty seafood, such as tuna or salmon.

Chia is another excellent food that provides omega-3 fatty acids.

Folic acid and vitamins B1 and B3 are found in brown rice. Additionally, low in glycemic index, brown rice releases glucose that gradually prevents blood sugar dips and mood fluctuations. These advantages are not present in instant rice varieties. Whenever you observe Steer clear of "instant" on a nutritional label.

Brewer's Yeast contains B1, B2, and B3 vitamins. Avoiding it is advised if you have trouble digesting yeast, try adding a thimbleful to any smoothie as your daily intake. This superfood has sixteen amino fourteen minerals and acids. Essential amino acids for the nervous system framework.

Ascorbic acid and folic acid are found in cabbage. Cabbage offers a defence against cardiac problems, infection, and tension. There are several methods to include cabbage in your diet via salads, wraps, stir-fries, and traditional

soups made with cabbage. Brazil nuts, black molasses, and raw cacao are examples of foods that are fantastic for crushing despair.

Additionally, while you're sad, you should avoid certain meals and chemicals. You need to abstain from smoking, coffee, and high-fat meals. as well as sugar. Keeping your blood sugar in check and getting your B vitamins is essentially for keeping your emotions in check.

Chapter 4

Adequate Sleep

Emphasizes the importance of getting enough rest.

Synopsis

Sleep gives you the mental fortitude you need to combat depression. You're more vulnerable to those negative signals circling in your brain when you don't get enough sleep. ability to take positive action on your behalf.

Relax

Ensure your bedroom is conducive to rest if you struggle with insomnia. It is meant to be a place of relaxation, not activity. Get rid of anything work-related and any other worries you may have, such as documentation and invoices. Should you maintain a computer or TV in your room, Transfer it to a different location. Make the minutes to combat despair. before having the most tranquil sleep of your life.

Cover digital clocks when it's time to turn out the lights; those radiant figures that always remind you of the time of day and the amount of sleep deprivation you're experiencing. Try your hardest to avoid all light sources; creating a completely dark environment is the aim. People who are fatigued exhibit increased irritability and moodiness. They are more likely to experience anxiety and sadness.

Generally speaking, an occasional insomniac night is not too problematic, although When sleep deprivation persists over time, several issues may arise. Every Lack of sleep influences your body's systems.

Find out why you're not getting enough sleep. Depression tension and worry might be the root of the issue; these concerns should be resolved and addressed. Your sleep apnea may be partially to blame for your awakening before the onset of REM sleep, keeping your eyes open and worn out.

It may also be something simple. Perhaps you should get a new mattress or find a better technique to make the room darker. Sounds might be keeping you awake. "White noise" may be needed because they are awake. That could be the whole of the preceding.

There will be some people who need medical attention. A physician should be seen for severe anxiety and depression. Regarding sleep apnea, the most effective course of action might be to do a sleep study. resolved. Many solutions exist, ranging from using a splint to prevent Your jaw shifted forward to certain breathing masks.

Herbal remedies for stress may be beneficial. Kava Kava is a wise selection. It cannot be taken consistently, and it is not advised while driving. Herbs that last longer include chamomile, lavender, Jasmine, and passionflower. For the sleeplessness itself, hops and valerian are useful. It may be possible to relieve mild to moderate depression with the wort of St. John. But be sure to use sunscreen as well. That herbaceous plant might make you more susceptible to light.

Try to establish a consistent schedule by going to bed and waking up at around the same time every day. Don't watch TV or read before bed. If you like coffee, make sure you just have one cup. just one or two in the morning. Exercise regularly might significantly aid in obtaining more sleep. When you're tired, consider you try not to take naps throughout the day. This only disrupts your sleep schedule.

The human body needs to sleep, so the sooner you

figure out what's preventing you from getting the

rest you need, the better.

Chapter 5

Exercise Even Though It's Difficult

Encourages physical activity despite challenges

Synopsis

Numerous studies have shown that being active and exercising may significantly reduce the symptoms of depression and improve the quality of life for those who experience it. depression. Even Nevertheless, the specific justifications for exercising having a positive effect on depression aren't entirely evident, the results are impressive.

Activities that use large muscle groups may be able to ease the symptoms of "repressed" anxiety. Moving, allowing for the complete range of motion, extending the muscles, and increasing circulation, among other things, may assist people in releasing stress and Anger. Physical fitness improves one's weight and overall look. This might undoubtedly contribute to elevating one's mood by increasing confidence and self-worth. People who work out usually experience an improvement in their sense of self-control. their lives, as well as their bodies. An aura of proficiency surrounds the Exercise and promotes better self-esteem. Exercise has been shown to create beta-endorphins, the body's natural analgesics that resemble morphine.

and a source of pleasure. This "feel good" feeling is often called "runner's high".

Exercise therapy is starting to gain traction. Several of Here are some benefits of exercising for depression:

1. People claim that they may think more clearly, feel happier, feel better about themselves, lose weight, gain strength, and experience a feeling of well-being when they exercise.

2. Physical activity increases happiness

3. They have better sleep.

4. Reduce nervousness and jitters,

5. Physical activity reduces melancholy

6. Work out with more vigour

7. Physical activity may contribute to a sense of greater coherence.

8. Engaging in exercise enhances the sense of social integration

When it comes to treating depression, exercise might be just as effective as or even more so than prescription medications. This is because exercise has no negative effects at all; in fact, it

has many health benefits. Additionally, the advantages of it are noticeable as soon as the first workout is completed on the brain. Exercise releases the body's natural analgesics, which are both nor-epinephrine and adrenaline, which are also known to act as enhancers of mood.

You can perform high-intensity exercises like running, kickboxing, spinning, and skipping rope.

If you find that running is too intense, you can start by walking and gradually work your way up to a brisk walk and eventually a slow walk. Run.

Make sure your mind is focused when you walk quickly. Be mindful of breathing, the surrounding environment, and your senses and body. Being relaxed and aware will assist you in overcoming anxiety and

depression. It will increase your cognitive function and mental clarity. of the area around you.

It's true that since your body isn't used to working out, the first day will be difficult. However, if you're still exhausted after working out for a week, there's a problem with your routine. Obtain expert assistance because a bad workout regimen is more detrimental than none.

Make sure you have a nutritious meal before working out. A glass of milk, some crackers, or an entire fruit are all healthy options. Never work out when you're hungry because it could increase your episodes of depression.

Chapter 6

Don't Drink:

Advises against excessive alcohol consumption.

Synopsis

Forty per cent of heavy drinkers exhibit symptoms similar to those of depression.

Nevertheless, when these same people abstain from alcohol 5% of men and 10% of women experience symptoms related to heavy meeting the criteria for a depression diagnosis - not that distinct from the spectrums of depression in the general population populace.

Avoid It

Five to ten per cent of people who suffer from depression also exhibit signs of alcoholism.

Depression and alcohol problems are very prevalent. They could take place entirely independently or in tandem. Alcohol is sometimes used by people who are depressed as a kind of self-medication, such as to try to make themselves feel better or occasionally to aid in falling asleep. Alcohol can temporarily improve mood in small doses, but when used to treat a depressive illness, problems arise. Taking it for depression treatment or not has a depressing effect on people's emotions.

Suicidal ideas can arise as a result of depression. Alcoholism's impulsivity, impaired judgment, and lack of self-control can make someone more likely to attempt suicide. Generally speaking, a significantly higher rate of suicide, both completed and tried, has a connection to alcohol.

Alcoholism and depression's fundamental issues are frequently complex. by social issues. Alcohol use can frequently result in issues at work the disease, a lack of functioning, or both. The demise of an A person's occupation negatively affects their financial situation. circumstances and household life. Troubles in marriage often stem from an alcohol problem, though it's unclear which started first.

Numerous physical issues can also be brought on by alcohol consumption. The body's organs are spared very few, if any. Heavy alcohol consumption is usually the cause of liver problems, which can manifest as jaundice from cirrhosis of the liver, hepatitis, or liver failure. These if left uncurled will result in death.

Certain antidepressants have sedative properties. When combined with alcohol, they can cause extreme sedation and put a person's breathing in danger. Furthermore, a variety of antidepressants are decomposed in the liver. Given that alcohol consumption may harm the liver, the amounts of these The amount of antidepressants in the bodies of those who are also heavy alcohol consumption. This could result in a rise in the negative effects of the drugs that fight depression.

Many of the symptoms that heavy drinkers report having are similar to those of depression, including:

- Exhaustion

- Disrupted sleep

- Waking up early

- Insufficient amounts of energy

- Not enough of an appetite

The situation is made more difficult by the possibility that depression can result from heavy alcohol consumption. It is therefore customary to address the alcohol problem before attempting to address the depression. Should it fail to do so, then a specific depression treatment plan would begin.

Use of selective serotonin reuptake inhibitors (SSRIs) for treatment Antidepressants may help with alcoholism as well as depression. This may indicate a shared cause of the two disorders.

Chapter 7

Don't Blame Yourself

Reminds readers not to be too hard on themselves.

Synopsis

Everybody has harmful thoughts occasionally, but if these thoughts are persistent and seriously affecting you, you need to take steps to manage your mind. concentrate.

Show kindness

Mental illnesses such as depression can be the source of constant anxiety, uncertainty, or pessimism. It could also result from a diet, from being under a lot of stress, or from the adverse effects of a medication. If the way you think is affecting your behaviour and mood around other people, you should consider what might be the underlying cause of this. As soon as you can identify that you have an issue, you should troubleshoot to find the most suitable fix. Remember that what works best for some people might not work for you when it comes to controlling mental behaviour.

Overcoming depression is challenging—possibly the most challenging thing you'll ever do. Fighting depression is a dogfight, not a stroll in the park.

However, you can prevail in the struggle if you decide to take up arms. Your thoughts are expressed through your emotions. You automatically change your emotions when you change your ideas. You don't need to struggle against the distorted and negative feelings that keep coming back to you. Instead, you must learn how to change your thought patterns, and emotions will naturally take care of themselves. Your emotions become healthy and positive when your views are positive, just as darkness follows light.

You will need to change your internal dialogue if you want to change how you feel. You will need to communicate with your brain differently. You exert positive pressure on your brain.

direction by focusing on positive and healthful ideas.

You can genuinely cultivate optimism if you fill your mind with enough positive ideas. Your life isn't lost, and you aren't bleak. The moment you start doing this, your life immediately gets better.

enlightening thoughts into your consciousness.
Combating depression is

fought in the area of concentration. You must develop the ability to firmly and consistently command your attention if you want to overcome depression.

Your perspective on things shifts when you change what you see. When you change the topics you cover or how you cover them modifications. When you change the items you think about, the way you Think about how things have changed. It genuinely matters what you believe how you talk about it, and what you take into consideration, as all of these things change who you are and transform you into a distinct person. You have to watch Think about

Good Things, talk about Good Things, and contemplate good things if

You want to overcome your depression and turn into a positive person.

People who are depressed adeptly ignore the facts, skipping over them and focusing instead on their emotions. They create consistent "facts" after fully immersing themselves in their emotions.

with those emotions. They approach problems pragmatically by thinking backwards.

You can't continue to believe that your emotions define you. Instead, you pivot the laws in place and assert that life's circumstances dictate how people feel about existence. You become an expert at gathering information and drawing conclusions. show that your emotions are in line with theirs. If emotions aren't yes, you disregard your emotions and accept the situation as it is until your emotions shift.

Chapter 8

See Someone

Encourages seeking professional help when needed.

Synopsis

The goal of cognitive behavioural therapy, also known as CBT, is to address issues with abnormal emotions, behaviours, and thoughts through a goal-oriented, methodical, focused procedure. The title appears in several methods for defining cognitive therapy and behaviour therapy and refers to treatmentsthat aret are founded on a

mix of standard behavioural cognitive

cognition.

Seek Assistance

Empirical evidence suggests that cognitive behavioural therapy (CBT) is effective in treating a variety of issues, such as mood, anxiety, personality, eating disorders, drug abuse, and psychotic disorders. For specific mental disorders, treatment is often provided using specific technique-driven, brief, direct, and time-limited interventions. Both group and individual therapy settings use CBT, and the techniques are regularly modified for self-help purposes. While some researchers and clinicians focus more on behaviour, others are more cognitive in their approach. Both are combined in other intercessions.

Before beginning cognitive therapy, you must understand the benefits of cognitive therapy for depression treatment. Will it be beneficial? to recover from depression? Cognitive therapy might be effective in many distinct ways. First of all, it provides the depressed person with counselling that is encouraging. This lessens the pain associated with depression. With the support of this therapy, the hopelessness that was likewise talked about. Overall, it leaves a lasting impression on the thoughts of the melancholy person.

A person experiencing depression appears to become more negative. Both the unrealistic expectations and the pessimistic thoughts can be changed with therapy. Critical self-evaluation can occasionally similarly lead to depression. This treatment might even enable you to do that.

This therapy aids the patient in realizing the difficulties in life, which are both minor and severe. The treatment attempts to create positive life objectives and foster a positive sense of self-worth in the person. When treating depression, cognitive therapy's benefits have been acknowledged by the majority of psychiatrists.

Several autonomous cognitive techniques include the following:

Writing automatically creates a mental distance between you and your harmful thoughts. Writing things down gives people perspective and makes it easier for them to recognize faulty thinking. If you find yourself in a situation where writing is simply not possible,. suggested saying things out loud.

Determine what's upsetting you. Just the simple fact that you own a place? Or did you sully your attire when you were changing it? or that, despite knowing you needed a new tyre, you chose not to replace it?

You might be sad that it needs to be replaced and irritated with the flat. dirty your outfit and were upset with yourself for forgetting to replace it in time. Thus, determine which themes are harmful. Regarding not changing the tire "I never stop. I'm not good at handling things on time. Concerning sullying the attire, "I'm a pig." I am unable to go anywhere and appear okay. Next, identify distortions and swap out irrational responses. Not every time do I stall. I balance my work and my family and carry out nearly every task that needs to be completed. "I am not a swine. I'm taking greater care than most with my appearance overall. people, which is why I find situations like these upsetting.

Next, discover distortions and replace rational

reactions."I don't always stall. I juggle my occupation and loved ones and execute just about everything that has to get done. "I'm not a pig. I'm generally really careful about my appearance, more so than most individuals, which is why affairs like this upset me.

Next, give the issue another look.

Do you still intend to go into an emotional meltdown? Most likely not. You're still not happy about getting the flat, though.

Finally, plan corrective action.

We're going to get that tyre as soon as I get off work. I have to grab some takeaway since that will take up the time I had intended to spend making dinner.

Wrapping Up

Even though depression is one of the worst diseases we have ever encountered, it is very treatable. Finding what works may take weeks, months, or sometimes even years of heartache and frustration. however, given the variety of choices we currently have, your chances are fantastic. Besides, we're not helpless onlookers. The choices we make to our lifestyles can significantly increase the likelihood that in our favour. If any of you are experiencing depression, please seek assistance. It should not be necessary for you to endure pain for more than one day. For those Do not give up hope if you are struggling with your treatments. An additional bright future is in store.